The Story of the
GETTYSBURG ADDRESS

By Kenneth Richards

Illustrated by Tom Dunnington

 CHILDRENS PRESS, CHICAGO

Library of Congress Catalog Card Number: 70-82962

5 6 7 8 9 10 11 12 13 14 15 16 17 18 19 20 21 R 79 78 77 76

It was the 1850's. The United States was in turmoil. The problem was slavery.

"Slavery is not right!" shouted the people of the North.

"We will do what we want in our own states!" answered the people of the South.

Tempers flared throughout the country. People were either for or against slavery. There seemed to be no middle ground.

The men in the Senate and the House of Representatives echoed the people's feelings. The floor of Congress became a battleground on which the North and South constantly clashed.

"Slavery should not be allowed in the new western territories!" said the northern congressmen.

"The federal government has no right to say that slavery will not be allowed in the territories!" the southern congressmen replied. "The people who live there should decide for themselves!"

The arguments went on and on. When it came time to elect a president in 1860, the country was confused and divided. There were four candidates for the presidency and each one had a different solution to the slavery problem. It did not seem possible that the people of the United States could stop arguing long enough to choose among them.

Abraham Lincoln was the Republican candidate. He traveled from state to state telling the people his views. "I will not abolish slavery where it already exists, but we must not let the practice spread," he said. "I am opposed to allowing slavery in the new territories."

The southern states did not like Lincoln's attitude toward slavery. "If Abraham Lincoln is elected president," they threatened angrily, "we will leave the Union!"

When Lincoln narrowly won the election, seven southern states held to their threat. Before the new president was inaugurated in 1861, South Carolina, Mississippi, Florida, Alabama, Georgia, Louisiana, and Texas seceded from the Union. They formed their own country, the Confederate States of America. Very soon, four more states joined them.

Anger mounted in the northern states. The people felt that the South had no right to leave the Union. But the southern states were firm. "The Union is an organization of independent states," they argued. "We chose to join it, and we can choose to leave it."

President Lincoln was worried. The United States was on the brink of war. "The Union must be saved," he said. He tried to think of a peaceful solution to the problem, but already the Confederacy had asked for the surrender of all federal forts within their territory. Then, on April 12, 1861, Confederate guns fired on

Fort Sumter in South Carolina, and the Civil War began.

It was a terrible war. Both armies were poorly clothed and badly fed, and there was little time to care for the sick and the wounded. In the first two years of fighting, thousands of men died on both sides. But worst of all, no side seemed to be winning. It appeared that the fighting would go on and on.

Then, early in the summer of 1863, frightening news spread throughout the northern states. It crackled along telegraph lines to Washington, D.C., New York, Philadelphia, and Boston. Newspapers printed special editions. Each had a huge, one-word headline — INVASION! Confederate General Robert E. Lee and his rebel army were invading the North!

General Lee had tried to fight his way north the year before, but he had been stopped at the Battle of Antietam in Maryland. This time he was determined to carry the war into Pennsylvania, and perhaps as far north as New Jersey and New York!

"Many people in the North are tired of fighting," Lee had reasoned. "Until now the major battles have been in the South, in Virginia and Tennessee. If we can carry the war to northern soil and threaten some of the large cities, perhaps the people will want peace. Then the South will have its independence. But first, we must win a great battle."

Day after day General Lee's army pushed farther north. The days were hot and the roads dusty. Many of the soldiers had no shoes. Still the long gray lines of Confederate troops kept moving. As they drew nearer, local militia units from towns in Pennsylvania and New York were called to duty. Armed with rifles and shotguns, old men and young boys left their farms and their jobs to defend their homes and the Union.

Afraid that the Confederates would attack Washington, D.C., the Union Army took up positions around the capital to defend it against the invaders. But Lee had other plans. He did not intend to attack Washington. Instead, he led his troops across Maryland and invaded Pennsylvania. He split his forces and soon the Confederates had captured several small towns and even threatened Harrisburg, the state capital.

General George G. Meade and thousands of blue-uniformed Union soldiers rushed to catch the Confederates. General Meade knew that Lee's forces were scattered. Union spies had told him that some units were as much as fifty miles away from Lee's headquarters. If General Meade could find the Confederate troops while they were still divided, he could defeat them easily.

Confederate scouts watched General Meade's movements. They sent word to General Lee that the Union Army was drawing closer. Lee realized that he had to gather his troops together quickly. Until now he had encountered little resistance, but soon he would have to make a stand. He studied a map of Pennsylvania, trying to find the best place to bring his soldiers together. At last he sent an order to all his field commanders, "Move your troops to Gettysburg!"

General Meade did not know that Lee's army was moving toward Gettysburg. But, in his efforts to find the Confederates, he had stationed a detachment of cavalry and two small infantry units outside Gettysburg to keep watch over the area. Early on the morning of July 1, 1863, the Union soldiers accidentally discovered a Confederate infantry brigade advancing toward the small, quiet country town. The Union troops opened fire and the Battle of Gettysburg began.

Soon General Lee arrived and took command of his men. The fighting grew intense as more and more

Confederate troops hurried to the scene and rushed into the battle. Gradually, the Union soldiers were forced to retreat back through the town to the top of a long hill called Cemetery Ridge.

When night fell, the Union men dug defensive positions on the ridge and on Culps Hill nearby. Soon General Meade arrived and called his commanders together to discuss strategy for the next day's fighting. Along the Union lines, the weary and hungry troops lay beside their guns, waiting for the morning and new Confederate attacks. During the night, thousands of reinforcements, both Blue and Gray, arrived on the battlefield.

With the sun's first rays on July 2, the battle began again. The Confederates had taken positions almost directly opposite the Union lines. Only a distance of 1400 yards separated the two armies. The people of Gettysburg huddled in their homes as horses and artillery rumbled through the streets. The town trembled to the thunder of cannon and the rattle of musket fire. At the end of the day nothing had changed. No matter where the Confederates had struck, the Union men held to their positions.

The third day of fighting was the worst. General Lee knew this would be his last chance to win the battle. His supply of ammunition was running low. Many of his men had been killed or wounded and there was no possibility of reinforcements. Realizing that the Union Army was in a strong position, he saw that his only hope lay in a direct frontal attack of the Union lines.

Carefully, Lee positioned his artillery and assembled his men for the final encounter. Then he gave the order to begin the attack. More than 140 Confederate cannon began to fire at the same time. The Union artillery on Cemetery Ridge returned the fire. For two hours, the guns on both sides exchanged murderous cannonades. Then, to conserve ammunition, the Union gunners stopped. The soldiers waited.

Suddenly, a line of Confederate soldiers, a mile long, emerged from the woods directly opposite the Union lines. With regimental banners flying, the Confederate soldiers advanced. The Union soldiers could not believe their eyes! The Rebels were marching across the open field, heading straight for the Yankee positions on Cemetery Ridge!

The Union troops opened fire and many Rebels fell. But still, the brave Confederates, led by General George Pickett, kept moving forward. The Yankees held their positions and did not retreat as the Confederates moved up the ridge. Suddenly, the two armies crashed together in hand-to-hand combat. Fierce fighting raged up and down the Union lines. The Yankees sent for more men to help repulse the attack, but the Rebels had no fresh troops on which they could call. Finally, the shattered Confederate ranks began to fall back. More than half of their men lay dead or wounded on the battlefield. The Battle of Gettysburg, one of the most important of the Civil War, was over. The Confederates had lost.

General Lee rode out to meet his tired soldiers as they returned from the fight. "It is all my fault," he said. "You have been brave men."

On July 4, 1863, the Confederates began their retreat South. The invasion was over. At Gettysburg the Confederacy had lost its chance to win a decisive battle and threaten the northern states. Although nearly two years of fighting remained, the people of the North now knew that the Union would be preserved.

After the armies had left Gettysburg, many people came to see the battlefield. Broken gun carriages, shattered muskets, dead horses, and rusting bayonets lay everywhere. Branches of trees had been shot away. Barns and farmhouses were in ruins, and fences broken.

Much livestock had been killed, and the wheat and cornfields trampled.

Even worse than this, however, were the thousands of shallow graves scattered all over the battlefield. Soldiers of both sides had been buried where they had fallen. In many cases, their comrades had carved rough crosses to mark the graves, but in the heat of battle there had been little time for a decent burial or funeral.

"Something must be done for our heroes," the people said. "We must find someplace to bury them with honor."

Mr. David Wills, a citizen of Gettysburg, had a plan. "We will make a new cemetery," he said. "It will be just for the soldiers who died in the battle. We will call it the Soldier's National Cemetery."

He wrote a letter to Governor Curtin of Pennsylvania and told him of his idea. Governor Curtin thought it was a good plan and so did the governors of many other states.

When Mr. Wills had won the Governor's approval, he immediately set to work. Each state whose men had fallen on the battlefield sent money. Soon there was enough to purchase seventeen acres of land. A spot was chosen on Cemetery Ridge next to the small town cemetery that had been there for years and given the ridge its name.

A special design was drawn for the new cemetery. It would be laid out in a half circle with the graves arranged in rows. Each state would have its own special section. All the men from New York would be placed in one section, those from Ohio in another, and so it would be for each state in the Union. A headstone would mark each grave. It would tell the man's name, his regiment and company, such as "Co. B, 16th Vermont Volunteers." If the soldier could not be identified, the headstone would simply say "Unknown."

Soon burial teams were carefully bringing the thousands of bodies to their new resting places. Trees and flowers were planted all around the cemetery.

When the work was finished, the townspeople were very pleased. The brave men who had died now had an honorable resting place. We must dedicate the cemetery," Mr. Wills said. "I will ask important people to speak at the ceremony."

A few days later, in Washington, D.C., President Lincoln received a letter from Mr. Wills. He asked the President to come to Gettysburg and make a speech at the dedication of the Soldier's National Cemetery.

President Lincoln was a very busy man. The war was still going on and many matters needed his close personal attention. It was very difficult for him to get away from Washington, even for a little while. But he knew, perhaps more than anyone, how important the

Battle of Gettysburg had been. He wrote Mr. Wills that somehow he would find the time to come to Gettysburg.

The night before he was to leave Washington for the dedication, President Lincoln began working on his speech. He knew that the main speaker at the ceremony would be Mr. Edward Everett of Massachusetts, the most famous orator in America. He realized that Mr. Everett would talk for a long time and that there would be other speakers, so Lincoln decided to make his speech very short. Because he was aware of the fact that newspapers all over the country would print his speech, he wanted it to be perfect. He worked for hours, writing and rewriting the sentences. When he had finished the first draft, he went to bed.

Early the next morning, the President boarded the special train that was to carry him and the other dignitaries to Gettysburg. As the countryside of Maryland and Pennsylvania rolled past his window, Lincoln thought of the war. He knew that peace would eventually come to the land and that the Union would remain strong and undivided because of the efforts of brave men like those buried at Gettysburg. "My speech does not express how deeply I feel about these men," he thought. "I must rewrite it. I want people everywhere to understand what freedom means to us and how much we owe to the brave soldiers who died at Gettysburg."

The train arrived in the small town just as the sun was setting. A carriage drove Mr. Lincoln to the home of Mr. Wills where he was to spend the night. Mr. Everett was a guest in the house also. After dinner, the President went to his room to work on his speech.

During the evening, a group of people came to sing for the President beneath his window. Lincoln opened the window to wave, and then he spoke a few words to the crowd that had gathered. When they left, he returned to his work.

It was past midnight before the speech was finished. Lincoln had written it on two pieces of lined paper. There were only 268 words. "It is what I would call a short, short speech," he said. Then he went to bed.

At eleven o'clock the next morning, November 19, 1863, the parade to the cemetery began. Congressmen, generals, and governors were in the procession and there were brass bands and military units. Mr. Lincoln rode on a handsome horse. He wore a black suit, white gloves, and his tall, black stovepipe hat.

Nearly every citizen of Gettysburg had come to see the parade and hear the speeches. The shops and the schools in the town were closed and thousands of people lined the streets to watch the procession pass. Billy and Jenny Gibbs stood in the midst of the crowd in front of their father's store. They were very excited because their father was going to take them to see and hear the President.

The parade wound slowly out of the town and up the road leading to the cemetery. Most of the people had never seen the President before. They cheered as he passed, and he waved his hand or nodded his head. Billy and Jenny waved, too, and Jenny was sure that Mr. Lincoln waved back to her. Then, Billy, Jenny, and their father joined the crowd following the procession to the ridge.

At last the parade reached the cemetery. A platform had been built for the speakers and decorated with red, white, and blue bunting. President Lincoln climbed the steps to the platform and took his seat in the front row. In the distance he could see the great battlefield. The sounds of fighting were gone now and autumn leaves covered the ground. There was peace at Gettysburg. A tear came to Lincoln's eye as he remembered the men who had fought and died here only four months before.

Holding tightly to his children's hands, Mr. Gibbs pushed forward through the crowd until the three of them stood directly in front of the speaker's platform. Now they would be able to see and hear everything clearly.

A band played to open the ceremony. When the music ended, the crowd grew silent as a minister said a prayer. Following the prayer, the United States Marine Band played and then, one after another, speakers rose from their seats to address the crowd. They told the people that the cemetery was a grand achievement and

that the nation was very proud of the citizens of
Gettysburg. Soon it was time for Mr. Everett to speak.

Mr. Everett had a powerful voice and even those
farthest from the platform could hear his words. He
spoke for nearly two hours. When he was finished, a
choir sang a hymn that had been written especially for
the occasion. At last, the President was introduced.

Lincoln rose slowly from his chair and put on his
steel-rimmed glasses. Billy and Jenny looked up at his
kindly, but careworn, face. When the crowd had grown
silent, the President began to read from the two
handwritten pages he held in his hand.

"Fourscore and seven years ago our fathers brought forth on this continent a new nation conceived in liberty and dedicated to the proposition that all men are created equal.

Now we are engaged in a great civil war testing whether that nation, or any nation so conceived and so dedicated, can long endure. We are met on a great battlefield of that war. We have come to dedicate a portion of that field as a final resting-place for those who here gave their lives that that nation might live. It is altogether fitting and proper that we should do this.

But, in a larger sense, we cannot dedicate, we cannot consecrate, we cannot hallow this ground. The brave men, living and dead, who struggled here have consecrated it far above our poor power to add or detract. The world will little note nor long remember what we say here, but it can never forget what they did here. It is for us the living rather to be dedicated here to the unfinished work which they who fought here have thus far so nobly advanced. It is rather for us to be here dedicated to the great task remaining before us — that from these honoured dead we take increased devotion to that cause for which they gave the last full measure of devotion — that we here highly resolve that these dead shall not have died in vain, that this nation under God shall have a new birth of freedom, and that government of the people, by the people, for the people, shall not perish from the earth."

The people applauded when the President's speech was finished. Then everyone joined in singing a hymn. A final prayer was said, and the ceremony ended. Mr. Lincoln mounted his horse, and he and the other dignitaries rode down the hill to the town.

As Billy and Jenny walked slowly homeward with their father, they wondered about the President's speech.

"What did President Lincoln mean when he said 'fourscore and seven years ago'?" asked Billy.

"Well," replied his father, "a score of years would be twenty, so fourscore and seven would be eighty-seven years. Can you tell me what year that was?"

Billy closed his eyes for a minute as he tried to do the arithmetic in his head. Jenny, who was two years older, found the answer first. "The year was 1776," she said, triumphantly. "That was the year the Declaration of Independence was written."

"That's right," said Mr. Gibbs. "It was that year that our nation was born, or as Mr. Lincoln put it, 'brought forth upon this continent.' Who do you suppose the President was referring to when he said 'our fathers?'"

"I know," answered Billy. "He meant George Washington, Benjamin Franklin, Thomas Jefferson, and all the other men who helped to found our country. But what did Mr. Lincoln mean when he said this war is testing our nation?"

"When our nation was born," Mr. Gibbs explained, "the fathers of our country created a new kind of government. It was founded on the belief that all men have an equal right to liberty and freedom. As Mr. Lincoln said, we have a government of the people, by the people, and for the people. In other words, we govern ourselves by free elections. Many people thought that our kind of government would not last very long. The Union must win this war if we are to prove that a nation founded on this principle can last."

Turning a corner, they saw the little white house in which they lived. Mr. Gibbs had repaired the fence that had been smashed by army wagons during the battle. But there were still holes in the barn where cannonballs had struck.

"I liked what Mr. Lincoln said about the soldiers," Jenny said. "I'm glad that he and the other important people came to dedicate the cemetery."

"Yes," answered Mr. Gibbs, "everyone did their best

to honor the soldiers today. But, as Lincoln said, we must not forget the reasons why they fought and died here. They gave their lives to save our government and our way of life. We must work even harder now for the same cause. Unless the Union wins the war, they will have died for nothing."

As they turned into their gate, Billy said, "President Lincoln said that the world won't remember his speech, but I'll never forget it."

"The President was not talking just to the people who were at the cemetery," Mr. Gibbs replied. "His speech will be printed in many newspapers tomorrow, so he was really speaking to the nation and to the world. But I think he also had in mind all the generations of Americans to come."

"The Civil War will end some day and the Union will be saved," said Mr. Gibbs confidently, "but there will be other troubles for America in the years ahead. Each time our nation is threatened, Americans will remember Lincoln's words."

The next day, newspapers around the country printed President Lincoln's address. Most praised what he had said. But there were some newspapers that had never liked Lincoln and were opposed to his presidency. They never approved of anything he said and printed unfavorable comments about the speech.

In Washington, the President read the newspaper reports. "The people are disappointed," he said. He still did not believe that his speech was very good. To his surprise, he received an admiring letter from Mr. Everett. The letter said, "I should be glad, if I could flatter myself that I came as near to the central idea of the occasion in two hours as you did in two minutes."

Lincoln replied in his usual modest way. He wrote, "In our respective parts, you could not have been excused to make a short address or I a long one. I am pleased to know that in your judgment, the little I did say was not entirely a failure."

President Lincoln wrote three more revisions of his address. These copies, along with his two original drafts, are still in existence today. The first draft, written in Washington, and the second written at the Wills' home in Gettysburg, are on display at the Library of Congress. One of the copies, written by Lincoln after his return to Washington, is owned by Cornell University. Another is in the Illinois State Historical Society Library, and the third is in the Lincoln Room of the White House.

The Gettysburg Address has become the most famous speech in our history. Lincoln's words have as much meaning today as they had for the people who listened to them that day, at Gettysburg. The day after the dedication, a Chicago newspaper wrote, "The dedicatory remarks of President Lincoln will live among the annals of men." And so they have.

Four score and seven years ago our fathers brought forth on this continent, a new nation, conceived in Liberty, and dedicated to the proposition that all men are created equal.

Now we are engaged in a great civil war, testing whether that nation, or any nation so conceived and so dedicated, can long endure. We are met on a great battle-field of that war. We have come to dedicate a portion of that field, as a final resting place for those who here gave their lives, that that nation might live. It is altogether fitting and proper that we should do this.

But, in a larger sense, we can not dedicate — we can not consecrate — we can not hallow — this ground. The brave men, living and dead, who struggled here have consecrated it, far above our poor power to add or detract. The world will little note, nor long remember what we say here, but it can never forget what they did here. It is for us the living, rather, to be dedicated here to the unfinished work which they who fought here have thus far so nobly advanced. It is rather for us to be here dedicated to the great task remaining before us — that from these honored dead we take increased devotion to that cause for which they gave the last full measure of devotion — that we here highly resolve that these dead shall not have died in vain — that this nation, under God, shall have a new birth of freedom — and that government of the people, by the people, for the people, shall not perish from the earth.

Abraham Lincoln.